The Silver Fountain
INN & TEA PARLOR

by

Pamela Pidgeon

Owner/Innkeeper

The Silver Fountain
Inn and Tea Parlor
Second Edition

Copyright © 2019 by Pamela Pidgeon
ISBN: 978-1-73233-364-2
Library of Congress PCN 2019934414

To contact the current innkeepers, please visit
silverfountain.com

To order a copy of this book, please visit
AMITYpublications.com

Resources: *Shoreliner Magazine*, April 1952 edition. Pictures
on the following pages are from an article published in this
magazine, showing the Inn being recognized as the "House
of the Month": Pages 11, 17, 19, 21, 25, 27, 29, 31 and 35.

Printed in the United States of America

Acknowledgements

We are immensely proud and grateful to have been successful along with our amazing and dedicated staff in turning The Silver Fountain Inn & Tea Parlor into a prosperous business. We are equally grateful to other local businesses and friends who have helped promote our establishment.

We would like to thank the many wonderful guests who have, and who will in the future, travel through our doors from all over the world, leaving fond memories, frequently exceeding our expectations.

We would also like to thank the many recent descendants of Frank and Mary Williams who have appreciatively added pictures and more memories for us to share. You are always welcome.

Jim & Pam Pidgeon, Innkeeepers

Dedication

To our five children, parents, siblings, many other
family members and close friends, some who
have "dug in the trenches" by playing different
roles here with us while on our new adventure,
and others who have lent emotional support,
encouragement and patience.

A special dedication to Jim from Pam for
encouraging and supporting her dreams,
while being the forever loving husband and father,
all-out handyman and amazing grounds keeper.

You are all deeply loved and treasured!

Contents

History

The Williams Family

Built in 1871, the beautiful three-story Mansard-roofed Victorian that is known today as The Silver Fountain Inn was originally owned by Frank and Mary Williams. Frank joined his father, Isaac B., in business, to form the I.B. Williams & Sons Manufacturing Co. Along with his brother, George, they catapulted their lace and belt-making factory into one of the largest, most successful businesses in Dover, New Hampshire.

The factory was eventually relocated to Orchard Street from its original location in the Cocheco Mills and became known as one of the largest and most prosperous businesses in this area.

Frank and Mary Williams

The I. B. Williams & Sons Manufacturing Co.

Frank and Mary had two daughters, Marguerite and Dorothy, both of whom married gentlemen named "Mr. Brown," although the two gentlemen were not related.

Marguerite and Philip C. Brown lived across the street at 98 Silver Street, which at one time was the Old Gaol, or "jail," and the site of the last public hanging in Dover.

Dorothy and Leroy H. Brown resided in the house next door, located at 107 Silver Street, until Dorothy's husband and both parents had passed away. She then moved back to her childhood home, 103 Silver Street, living there until her death in 1977.

Frank Bartlett WILLIAMS
b. 22 Aug 1850, Dover, Strafford, NH (VR)
d. 31 October 1920, Dover, Strafford, NH (VR)
& Mary Elizabeth LOCKE
b. 23 Aug 1852, Salmon Falls, Strafford, NH
d. 24 Dec 1946, Dover, Strafford, NH
m. 16 Sep 1874, Dover, Strafford, NH

Marguerite Louise WILLIAMS
b. 4 Jun 1884, Dover/Boston
d. 19 Jun 1981, Dover, Strafford, NH
& Philip Carter BROWN
b. 27 Aug 1885, Dover, Strafford, NH
d. 17 Feb 1960, Clearwater Beach, FL
m. 1 Jun 1909, Dover, Strafford, NH

Dorothy Locke WILLIAMS
b. 20 Sep 1892, Dover/Boston
d. 3 Oct 1977, Dover, Strafford, NH
& LeRoy Hussey BROWN
b. 21 Apr 1891, ? Dover, Strafford, NH
d. 29 Sep 1944, Dover, Strafford, NH
m. 01 Jun 1920, Dover, Strafford, NH

Dorothy spent most of her school and college years in Massachusetts. She also traveled the world extensively, both before and during her marriage.

Most notably Dorothy was a Red Cross Volunteer in the 1917 Great Halifax Explosion off Nova Scotia, Canada, where a Norwegian vessel, the SS IMO, collided with the SS Mont-Blanc, a French cargo ship laden with high explosives, which killed 2,000 and injured another 9,000.

Throughout her life she held many civic positions, which included serving on the Board of Managers of the Colonial Dames in New Hampshire. She also was a manager for the Dover Children's Home; founded in 1893, it still exists today.

Canteen life in Halifax, N.S.
October 15th – December 23rd, 1918

Dorothy Brown – 1940

In 1952, the home at 103 Silver Street was chosen as "House of the Month" for the April edition of the *Shoreliner* magazine. The article included several photographs of the home's fine décor and post-Civil war style, most of which is still intact and original, speaking highly for the craftsmen and workmanship of the home.

Feature writer Justine Flint Georges stated that "the spacious and imposing Victorian house reminds one of all the gay yet quiet life typified after the war ... of leisurely rides with horse and fancy carriage ... of lawn parties on summer afternoons ... ladies in flowery silks and laces ... a comfortable, unhurried way of life that seems to have disappeared in the mists of time."

The Birth of the Bed & Breakfast

In the late 1980s, the beautiful home at the corner of Silver and Cushing Streets became known as The Silver Street Inn, owned and operated by Lorene L. Cook.

In the early 2000s, it was re-opened as a bed and breakfast by Janice Cotter and Michael Griffin and renamed The Williams House Inn. Unfortunately, the concept of B&Bs and social media had yet to take hold in the United States, making it difficult for the Inn to survive. It returned to single family ownership several times.

In 2005, this beautiful home was once again on the market. The threat of a new buyer stripping it down and turning it into condos or apartments, like many other historical homes in the surrounding area, was a real possibility.

Luckily, local resident and interior designer Susan Chang fell in love with the home and took on the challenge of transforming it into a successful bed & breakfast, which she named The Silver Fountain Inn.

As a former restaurant owner, Susan was able to utilize her talents in hospitality and design to revitalize the building and the business. Restoring the home's elegance and integrity, she created an inviting and memorable experience for her guests, as others did before her. Her passion and efforts forged a thriving business, and the Inn became well known in the community as *the* place to stay in Dover.

Susan's love for and dedication to The Silver Fountain Inn was ever present, even up through her diagnosis with cancer and subsequent passing in 2011.

The Silver Fountain Inn

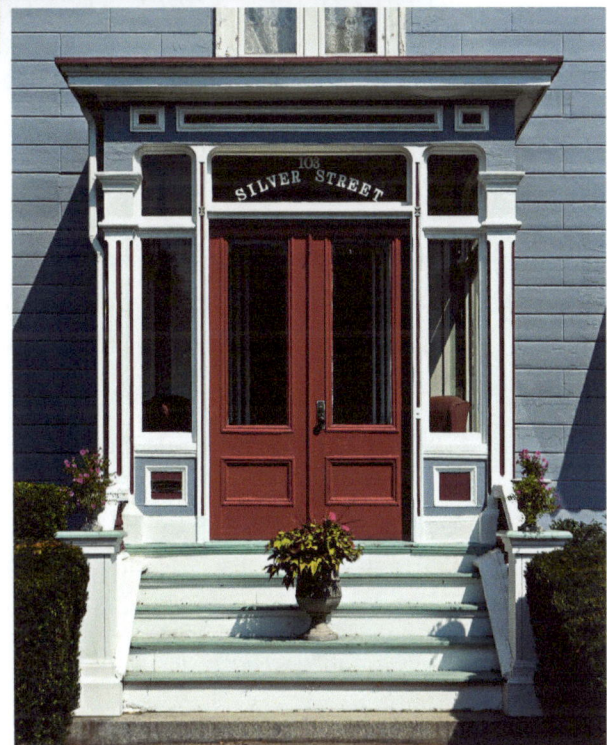

The Silver Fountain Inn

❦

The house originally had a 51 Cushing Street address, but Mary Williams petitioned the town to change it to Silver Street because that was known as where "the wealthy lived," due to the number of silver merchants who had originally resided there in Dover's early days.

Before the change of address, the main entrance, made of brick and granite, opened on Cushing Street. That doorway became the side porch, and a new entrance was built facing Silver Street.

Both the original and the later entryways feature foyers with large mahogany doors, slate floors, marble baseboards and decorative leaded glass panels.

The original foyer directly entered *The Parlor* which immediately captures one's attention with its beautiful Italian carved plaster ceiling, Appointed with Belgian light fixtures, the room features Honduran mahogany paneling encasing a French Caen sandstone fireplace and a handsome, large bookcase, all set off with Austrian hand-cut crystal doorknobs.

Secreted in the left-hand side of the fireplace paneling is a built-in bar complete with liquor spindle, sliding copper plate and a hidden compartment purported to be where Mary hid her purse and valuables, perhaps meant to also hide other bottled treasures during prohibition.

The Parlor

Walking through *The Hallway* to the dining room one can't help but stop and admire the hand-painted canvas done in the French style, *trompe l'oile*.

Painted in a floral and lattice design to match the carved plaster ceiling above it, the canvas is executed in varying shades of gray, masterfully spanning all three stories of the grand hallway and landings.

The Hallway

Like the hallway, the dining room has high paneled wainscoting topped by imported wallpaper with hand airbrushed birds and roses (leaving no two birds exactly the same), and includes another sand-stone fireplace.

The original table had a butler's bell that rang in the adjacent pantry, along with several other chimes that signaled for service in other areas of the home. A double dry sink, with a mahogany top and leaded glass cabinet fronts that run from top to bottom, provides additional areas of storage.

The dining room of the past is now an inviting *Sitting Room* for the guests.

The Sitting Room

The butler's pantry is the gateway between the dining room and the kitchen, which is the one room in the house that has been updated several times over the years for efficiency.

However, several features remain, like the cold storage cabinet and back servants' staircase. A small room off the kitchen was originally the servants' dining area; today it is used as an office. There is also a half bath and mud room, plus stairs leading down to the basement.

Even the basement here is quite grand and considerably modern, with its poured floors surrounded by massive blocks of granite.

The basement is made up of several different rooms – a canning room complete with the old canning cupboards; a clothes drying room; a coal room, including a sixteen-foot coal stove with coal drop; a furnace room; and a large, finished room complete with heat and electricity.

The basement also includes another bathroom meant for the coal tender, to avoid black ash and dust being spread throughout the house.

The Guest Rooms

Wandering back upstairs off the formal dining room is our king room, now known as *The Chamber*. Grand and richly appointed in warm peach and gold tones, this is our largest room, with a king-size canopied bed, a double day bed, a cherry wood leaf armoire, a large full bath, an electric fireplace, a desk and two sitting chairs. Located on the first floor, this room has its own private entrance with handicap accessibility.

Originally the wall behind the large canopied bed was not there. The large sun room with the many windows that encircled it was split into this room and its bathroom, plus the bathroom for The Boudoir.

This was one of Dorothy's favorite rooms and once housed pieces of memorabilia from several Asian and European countries collected by her son, David Williams Brown, who served in the military.

The Chamber

27

"Glide," as the Victorians might have said, through the hall to the front of the first floor and encounter the very ornate and beautiful *Boudoir Room*. Once known as the Music Room, family members often gathered here for an aperitif after dinner and musical entertainment. The doorway was originally wider, and drapes made of soft shades of rose, green and gold satin brocade identical to the silk walls, once completed the entrance in the French decorative theme of Louis XVI.

Today, The Boudoir Room features elegant pink silk wall coverings, beautiful custom moldings, a non-working French sandstone fireplace with a facing of onyx marble, antique brass candelabras, a dark cherry armoire and bureau, a divan, a Victorian vanity set, plus a walk-in shower.

The beauty of The Boudoir Room has been featured as a background for magazine publications such as *Shutterfly*, *Benjamin Walk* and *New Hampshire Wedding Magazine*.

The Boudoir

Traveling up the black walnut staircase to the second floor landing, following as the hand-painted canvas continues, one cannot help but be awestruck by the sheer volume surrounded by decorative moldings.

The second floor is where the main household members' bedrooms were once located. *The Dorothy Brown* is offered as a two room suite. Originally referred to as the Master Suite, this room is now the living room of that suite.

Originally the bedroom of the old Master Suite.

Today the living room of The Dorothy Brown Suite

The morning room, originally adjacent to the main bedroom, was kept warm by the brass Franklin-type stove, which is still in the room. This room now serves as a bedroom.

Originally the morning room of the old Master Suite.

Today the bedroom of The Dorothy Brown Suite

One of the three remaining second floor rooms, *The Marguerite* sits directly to the left at the top of the stairs. A large queen room with decorative rich moldings in pearl gold, green and rose patterned tones, it features an original antique headboard, a rose settee and the former cedar linen closet.

The second original subway-tiled bathroom resides on this floor as well.

The Marguerite

Intricately patterned parquet floors are found throughout the second floor bedrooms, with the exception of *The Henrietta,* which was originally the sewing and linen room, and in later times belonged to the cook, Viola. Servants' stairs can still be seen in this small chamber.

This second-floor bedroom is quaint and cozy, decorated in warm tones of rose, chocolate and cream, which collectively lend to a warm atmosphere. It features a queen-size bed, a large bureau, a side table, sitting chair and full bath with shower.

The Henrietta

Around the corner at the bottom of the third-floor stairway is *The Duchess*. This room features a queen-size canopied bed appointed in red and white toile, an antique vanity, a queen's chair, beautiful wooden parquet flooring, a shower bath and a white chaise lounge.

The Duchess

The four rooms on the third floor originally housed servants – three maids and a chauffeur, which is why they were not photographed in the 1952 article. The third floor stairs are noticeably smaller and steeper. The oak flooring now present throughout these rooms was once wide pine plank. The linen closet was originally a shared bath for the servants; now each room has its own private bathroom.

These four rooms all have their own décor. *The Duke* is stately and relaxing, decorated in deep natural tones with a matching carved mahogany queen bed, large dresser and mirror, filigree desk, and an oversized cushioned sitting chair with ottoman, plus bath with a shower.

The Eleanor is bright and sunny, decorated in blue and white cottage grace, with a queen bed, armoire, desk, wicker storage bench and chairs, and an electric wall fireplace, plus bath with shower.

The Duke

The Eleanor

The Vivienne features a queen-sized bed with an accent duvet, a desk, a sitting chair, plus an extra single daybed, decorated in soft mint and tan tones with garden accents. It also includes a fully contained bath with shower.

The English Rose, appointed in yellow and blue French country charm and appeal, is light and cheery, with a queen-size bed, an oak dresser and two chairs, plus private bath and shower.

The Vivienne

The English Rose

The Present

James and Pamela Pidgeon

The Innkeepers

On July 1, 2013, James and Pamela Pidgeon took ownership of The Silver Fountain Inn and are the current innkeepers of the home. In Pamela's words:

Jim and I are basically Seacoast natives. Jim had owned his own linen company for several years and now works for Johnson and Johnson. I had twenty-two years of experience working for UPS. Although we had a sound business knowledge, we had no experience in hospitality.

But we knew this was a rare opportunity to make a dream a reality. We loved to entertain, so decided to combine that with our business acumen, understanding we would have to raise occupancy and revenue by offering our guests a unique experience with superior service.

The Tea Parlor

While the Seacoast area is a sought-after destination from May through October, we quickly realized our first November to April season would be tough financially as occupancy falls off quite drastically. It was clear to us that we needed to find another way to raise revenue.

That first November, my mother invited me to tea with her and friends in Maine. It was then that the idea of creating a tea room started to form. I immediately went home that night and started researching menus, demographics and competition. I already knew that I had a built in ambience, and that serving lunch would fit perfectly with the bed and breakfast hours' needs. All that would be required would be a variance from the town to allow the public to be served lunch.

The town was very supportive in granting the variance. The Tea Parlor was opened by January, 2014, and has since been steadily growing. Our catchment area now reaches most parts of New England and consists of many varying crowds: Red Hat chapters, church groups, book clubs, and of course, friends simply enjoying each other's company over lunch.

Our atmosphere is unhurried, elegant yet casual – or as fancy as one might want, with hats and feather boas. We have also become a perfect venue for wedding and baby showers, plus birthday, graduation and retirement parties.

The Silver Fountain Inn's Tea Parlor is open Monday through Saturday, from 11:30 a.m. to 4:00 p.m.

The menu changes monthly to be able to offer the variety of different recipes and tastes that make a high tea so special. It ranges from lighter fare, such as sandwiches, salads, quiche and soup, to our fancy three-tiered "Duchess," which offers a sampling of tea sandwiches, scones with fresh Devonshire cream and lemon curd, miniature desserts, plus – of course – over thirty flavors of our fine tea.

The Tea Parlor

The "Duchess"

Special tea events are held with themes such as the Downton Soirée, Mother's Day, Valentine's Day, Christmas Holiday, Jane Austen, Tea Readings, Harry Potter and more.

The Chandelier

Tea Cup Holder

"Tea" Setting

51

With the advent of the Internet and social media, The Silver Fountain Inn now has guests from all over the nation and world. Some travelers are here for vacation and sightseeing, while others are visiting relatives, attending weddings or in the area for business.

And the Inn isn't just known for overnight accommodations. The Silver Fountain Inn and Tea Parlor was asked by New Hampshire Public Television to host a special tea for the final episode of the Downton Abbey series, held at The Rochester Opera House.

In addition, the Inn was voted "Editor's Choice for Best Tea Experience" in 2016 May/June issue of *Yankee* magazine's "Best of New England" series. It has also been listed as one of the "55 Best New Hampshire Getaways" by *Vacation Idea* magazine for 2016.

New Hampshire Public Television's Downton Abbey event.

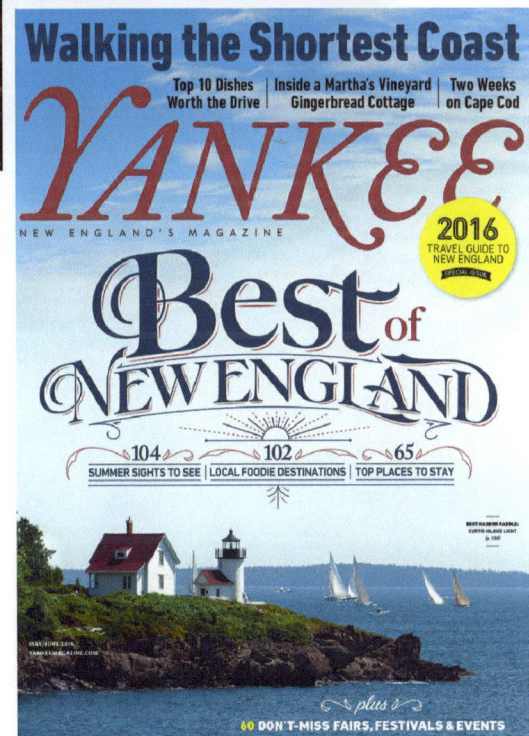

2016 Best of New England

Interior Décor

Our interior is complimented by several beautiful works of art created, and for purchase, by fellow Dover resident, Pete Dixon, who says, "I started what I call my 'Great Art Adventure' late in life, and I now paint to fulfill my lifelong dream of becoming an artist. I love painting people. People are what it's all about. I particularly like artwork from the Victorian era. I'm grateful to the owners of the Silver Fountain Inn for giving me a beautiful venue to share my work with others. Life is good!"

Our bookcases also display several other quality items from local artists, including jewelry, doll clothes, fairy houses and headbands, teapots and loose leaf teas, plus a number of products from the local purveyor Stonewall Kitchen.

Cupid

Melancholy Lady

Accolade

Blue Boy

The Gardens

One area we look forward to improving upon is the outdoors—the outside seating and gardens that surround the home to form a welcoming, peaceful retreat.

The massive tree, a hybrid of oak and maple that sits at the far corner of the parking lot, was here long before the house was built. The rhododendron off the side porch was planted shortly after the main entrance was moved.

A variety of perennials grace the grounds through the growing season. Among those favored are the purple wisteria vines on the front arbor, and the deep blue hydrangeas on the posts and surrounding the fountain.

The Side Porch

The Garden Swing

The Arbor

The Brick Lattice

The Carriage House

Once touted to "house a prize team of thoroughbreds and some of the most beautiful carriages in Dover," the carriage house over the years fell into despair. Recently, however, it has been totally renovated by Brothers Design, and reopened in November of 2018, featuring owners' living quarters upstairs and an elegant function room downstairs.

The owners living quarters features an open concept style, keeping the original beams and creating custom pieces from the original wood planks. The original cupola has been entirely restored, complete with lighting and a weathervane.

The function room has a capacity for sixty people and will comfortably host bridal and baby showers, intimate weddings, elopements and rehearsal dinners, parties celebrating birthdays and anniversaries, bereavement luncheons, business meetings and many of our own special events.

Left to right, Marguerite Williams, three of her college roommates, and Mary Elizabeth and Frank Bartlett Williams. In the back, Percy, the driver. 1908.

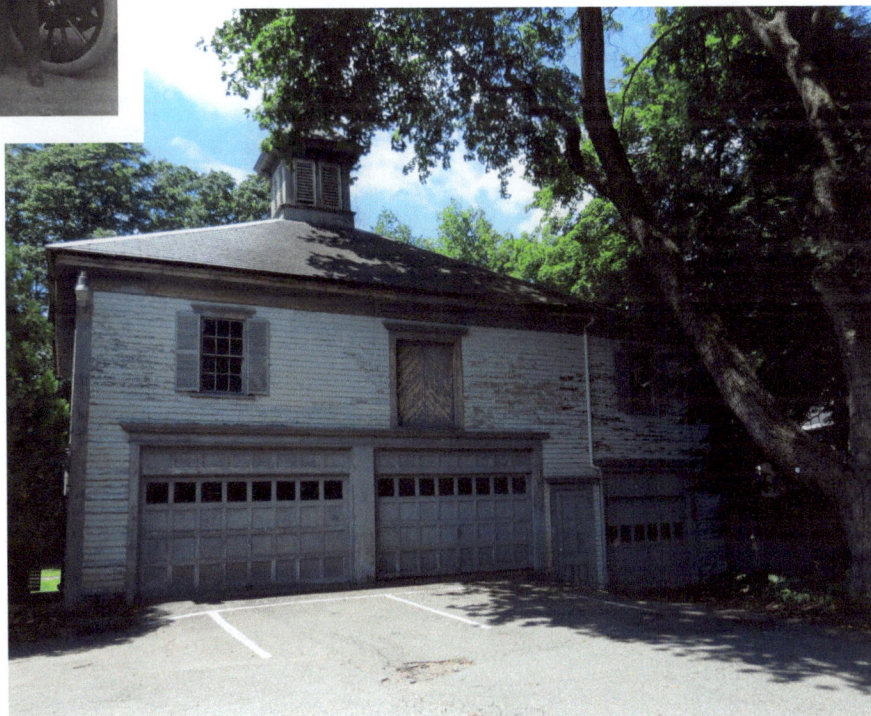

The Carriage House as it appeared before its renovation that was completed in 2018.

The renovated

Carriage House

The Function Room

Special Events

Besides our Tea Events, special dinner events are held at The Silver Fountain Inn and Tea Parlor, including themed dinners and Murder Mystery Weekends.

Our theme dinners usually include an intimate performance by local acting groups like Vagabonds Productions, Theatre Unmasked and the Garrison Players, along with a paired five-course dinner. Among others, these evenings have included such shows as *A Night in Downton Abbey*, *A Christmas Carol* and *Dracula*.

Carolers

The full cast of
Downton Abbey, *2015*

Tim Robinson as Scrooge, 2015

The Garrison Players A Christmas Carol *cast, 2018*

Our Murder Mystery Weekends have become quite a niche, not only for us but for our guests as well. Our murder mystery dinners are unlike those where guests simply watch and experience little, if any, participation.

Our version is considered a live game of "Clue" in that the guests are actually the characters. They are welcome to join other guests for a night of extortion, bribery and murder, or make it even more fun by getting their own group together.

We also offer the perfect venue for a birthday party, "girls" weekend, bachelorette party, team building office party or rehearsal dinner. Our goal is to offer a fun, relaxing and memorable experience for all our guests.

We present several different themes, from Westerns, medieval, Roman, pirate, rich & famous, 1920s, '50s, 'and 70s, to Margaritaville and many more.

Murder of a Millionaire

Terror in a Toga

Murder Among the Mateys

Spring and summer offer lovely opportunities for outdoor wedding pictures. With several backdrops and areas to choose from, all the tulip and iris bulbs take their turns adding color to the already luscious green lawn and classical setting.

※∾(⟨⟩)∾※

www.ingramcontent.com/pod-product-compliance
Lightning Source LLC
Chambersburg PA
CBHW041426090426
42741CB00002B/43